TEEN CHALLENGES

SOCIAL MEDIA AND DIGITAL STRESS

by Kaitlyn Duling

CONTENT CONSULTANT

Marguerite Ohrtman, EdD, LPCC, NCC, ACS
Director of School Counseling
Director of Clinical Training
University of Minnesota

Essential Library

An Imprint of Abdo Publishing | abdobooks.com

ABDOBOOKS.COM

Published by Abdo Publishing, a division of ABDO, PO Box 398166, Minneapolis, Minnesota 55439. Copyright © 2022 by Abdo Consulting Group, Inc. International copyrights reserved in all countries. No part of this book may be reproduced in any form without written permission from the publisher. Essential Library™ is a trademark and logo of Abdo Publishing.

Printed in the United States of America, North Mankato, Minnesota.
102021
012022

THIS BOOK CONTAINS
RECYCLED MATERIALS

Cover Photos: Shutterstock Images, foreground, background
Interior Photos: ArtistGNDphotography/iStockphoto, 4; Tom Wang/Shutterstock Images, 8; Shutterstock Images, 10, 37; iStockphoto, 14, 20, 22–23, 24, 50, 68, 71, 78–79, 80, 89, 90, 98–99; Paul Sakuma/AP Images, 28; Rosdiana Ciaravolo/Getty Images Entertainment/Getty Images, 31; SolStock/iStockphoto, 38; Antonio Guillem/Shutterstock Images, 45; Rawpixel.com/Shutterstock Images, 46; McLittle Stock/Shutterstock Images, 55; Darren Baker/Shutterstock Images, 56; Tero Vesalainen/iStockphoto, 60; Monkey Business Images/iStockphoto, 66–67, 74; New Africa/Shutterstock Images, 83; Monkey Business Images/Shutterstock Images, 96

Editor: Katharine Hale
Series Designer: Colleen McLaren

LIBRARY OF CONGRESS CONTROL NUMBER: 2021941248

PUBLISHER'S CATALOGING-IN-PUBLICATION DATA

Names: Duling, Kaitlyn, author.

Title: Social media and digital stress / by Kaitlyn Duling

Description: Minneapolis, Minnesota : Abdo Publishing, 2022 | Series: Teen challenges | Includes online resources and index.

Identifiers: ISBN 9781532196294 (lib. bdg.) | ISBN 9781098218102 (ebook)

Subjects: LCSH: Social interaction in adolescence--Juvenile literature. | Stress in youth--Juvenile literature. | Social problems in mass media--Juvenile literature. | Social media and society--Juvenile literature.

Classification: DDC 302.231--dc23

CONTENTS

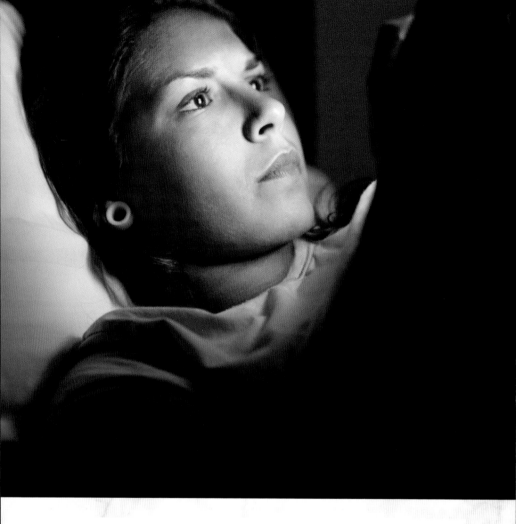

Some teens are on digital devices and social media late into the night.

CHAPTER ONE

TECHNOLOGY OVERLOAD

Breanna's phone vibrated with an aggressive *Bzzz*. The phone's screen lit up, emitting a soft, blue glow in the pitch-black darkness of her bedroom. She rolled over, still half asleep, and saw several green icons. Breanna had notifications—lots of them. She quickly tapped through the apps, noting comments and updates from her best friends, as well as some from strangers or people she had met online. After reading the comments and checking the likes on her latest Instagram selfie, Breanna scrolled through dozens of photos on the app. She had gone to bed early, trying to get some sleep before the next morning's biology final, but that wasn't working out as well as she'd hoped. Her friends were blowing up her phone with texts and comments. When the texting slowed, Breanna mindlessly checked her other apps over and over. She had posted the selfie a couple of hours ago and was now watching the number of likes go up. This made her feel good, but she was still hoping, nervously, that her crush might leave a comment on it.

Breanna yawned and frowned. The photos on social media were giving her serious FOMO—fear of missing out. Some girls from school were posting throwback pictures of their spring break trips from last week, showing off their fashionable outfits and rowdy beach parties. Breanna hadn't been allowed to go on a beach trip this year. Scrolling through, she saw her cousin's new puppy, Boomer, and instantly felt jealous. Breanna wanted a puppy more than anything in the whole world. Judging by what they posted on social media, everyone but her seemed to have cool clothes, fun vacations, cute puppies, or even new cars.

Then she saw a picture that immediately made her stop scrolling. Her friend Jazz was at a party with the basketball team. The guy Breanna had a crush on was in the photo. Breanna immediately felt sick to her stomach and couldn't stop wondering why she wasn't invited. Annoyed and agitated, she threw down her phone, but that didn't mean she was going to sleep. The persistent *Bzzz* of the smartphone kept her checking her notifications late into the night.

DIGITAL OVERLOAD

At school the next morning, Breanna slumped at her desk, totally exhausted. A huge yawn escaped from her mouth just as Mr. Lane stepped in front of the class. "Sleepy again, Breanna? Do we need to have a talk about your ability to stay awake and alert in my class?"

FOMO

The popular phrase FOMO stands for "fear of missing out," and it describes situations in which a person fears missing out on fun and exciting social events that friends and acquaintances might be experiencing. In the context of social media, a case of FOMO can lead someone to check his phone or other device constantly in an effort to keep tabs on what others are doing. It can also lead people to obsess over the lives of others while missing out on their own experiences.

FOMO can feel like a deep sense of jealousy. It is often worsened by sites such as Instagram and Facebook that often show only the best moments of others' lives. At its worst, FOMO can affect a person's self-esteem, anxiety levels, and mood.

Breanna, now embarrassed *and* exhausted, just frowned and shook her head. It was time to pair up and work on their partner projects, so she scooted her desk over to Sasha's.

Overuse of digital devices can interfere with sleep, causing fatigue and poor concentration.

"Bre, you need to focus up," Sasha said, already jotting down a list in her notebook. "I need an A on this project, and I am not going to let you mess that up. Is everything OK? Mr. Lane is right; you've been so sleepy and grumpy lately."

Breanna's brow furrowed as she laid her head down on her desk. "It's nothing; I'm fine," she said. "I just stayed up too late last night."

Sasha poked her friend with a pencil and teased, "Checking out Jay's Instagram again, huh?"

A half smile grew on Breanna's face, but she shook her head, saying, "Yeah, some, but mostly I've just been scrolling. Seeing how many likes I get. Some of the girls in my homeroom are getting famous online. They get thousands of likes, and they look *so* cool, like models or actresses. I just want to get on their level, you know?"

As Mr. Lane stopped by to check on the girls' work, Sasha and Breanna scrambled to look busy, then started whispering again as he walked past. "Listen," Sasha said. "I know what you're saying. Sometimes I get way too invested in what's happening on my social media. But don't you know that everyone uses filters and edits their photos? What we see on social media isn't real. Getting an A on this project is what's real."

Breanna rolled her eyes and laughed, but Sasha persisted. She said, "I'm your best friend, right? Try something with me. Let's turn off the notifications on our social media. Instagram, Facebook, Twitter . . . everything. Then we can set a schedule: we look at the apps once at lunchtime and once after dinner. But then the phone is for texting only. No social media and no notifications. Maybe if we set some boundaries, both of us can start to feel better. Want to try it?" Breanna started to roll her eyes again, but then she remembered how tired she was and how bad she

Some people delete social media apps to remove the temptation to check their phone constantly.

had felt last night when she couldn't measure up to the people on her feed. She said, "Well . . . I could try. At least for a few days, right?" Sasha punched the air with her fists and did a dance in her seat, exclaiming, "Yes! Now let's get back to this project and get me an A."

REAL LIFE

Breanna's experience is not unusual. Teens and tweens across the United States are consuming more digital media than ever before, and smartphone ownership continues to rise, keeping teens connected to the internet 24 hours a day. Common Sense Media is a nonprofit group that provides parents and schools with recommendations for age-appropriate entertainment and technology. A survey the group conducted found that 84 percent of teens ages 13 to 18 owned a smartphone in 2019, and 19 percent of eight-year-olds had their own smartphone too.[2] Screens, the internet, and social media are all standard parts of day-to-day life for today's kids and teens.

THE DIGITAL DIVIDE

Significant disparities exist when it comes to device ownership. These disparities are known as the digital divide. In 2019, children from higher-income homes were more likely than those from lower-income homes to have a personal laptop, smartphone, or desktop computer at home. About 94 percent of eight- to 18-year-olds in higher-income households had access to a computer at home, while only 73 percent of children in lower-income households had access.[3] While the digital divide narrowed between 2015 and 2019, the divide in ownership and access remains.

With all of that screen time, teens, tweens, and young adults watch videos, send text messages and emails, browse websites, and use social media. Social media platforms and apps such as Instagram, TikTok, Twitter, Facebook, and others have exploded in popularity, becoming must-haves for adolescents. These tech tools

SCREEN TIME: BY THE NUMBERS

The phrase *screen time* refers to the amount of time spent using a screen, be it on a phone, tablet, computer, television, or other device. Researchers have long debated what constitutes a healthy amount of screen time at different ages and stages of development. The experts haven't come to a consensus, but they do know that teens spend a large portion of their days on screens. In fact, almost three out of ten teenagers spend more than eight hours per day using screen media. The average amount of daily screen time for teens is seven hours and 22 minutes, which is almost half of a teen's waking hours.[5] The figure does not include screens used at school or for homework, which would boost these numbers even higher.

help teenagers connect with others, express themselves, discover new ideas, and have fun. But they can also cause problems. While many of these tools and apps are enjoyable, high amounts of screen time can be linked to increased anxiety, depression, and emotional instability in teenagers. A 2018 study found that both moderate use of screens (four hours a day) and high use of screens (seven hours a day) are associated with lower psychological well-being than just one hour of use a day.[4] The study included children ages two to 17 and found larger links between well-being and screen time in adolescents than in children. Jean Twenge, one of the study's authors, said, "At first, I was surprised that the associations were larger for adolescents. . . . However, teens spend more time on their phones and on social media, and we know from other research that these activities are more strongly linked to low well-being than watching television and videos, which is most of younger children's screen time."[6]

In ways both big and small, social media and other digital tools are having negative effects on teens' lives— but the situation isn't hopeless. Researchers are working to determine the underlying causes of digital and social media stress, to learn why social media can be especially problematic for teens, and to develop solutions that will help teens build healthy relationships with technology and social media.

"EDUCATORS AND PARENTS ARE STRUGGLING WITH HOW TO MAKE SENSE OF THIS NEW WORLD AND HOW TO EMPOWER KIDS TO USE TECHNOLOGY RESPONSIBLY TO LEARN, CREATE, AND PARTICIPATE—IN OTHER WORDS, HOW TO BE DIGITAL CITIZENS."[7]
—JIM STEYER, COMMON SENSE MEDIA, 2019

Cell phones and other mobile devices have made it easy and convenient to access information such as recipes.

CHAPTER TWO

WHAT IS DIGITAL STRESS?

In addition to the physical world, most people today are also residents of the digital world. This world is accessed using computers and other devices that are connected to one another over the internet. Technology has become a constant presence in modern life. According to a 2018 survey by the Pew Research Center, almost all US teens (95 percent) said they have access to a smartphone, even if they do not own one themselves. In the same survey, 45 percent of US teens said they are "almost constantly" on the internet.[1] Many teenagers said they check for messages and notifications first thing in the morning. Teens and young adults aren't the only ones who have high rates of technology use, as studies show that 81 percent of US adults own smartphones and about 74 percent own a desktop or laptop computer.[2]

This digital world offers plenty of opportunities for communication, learning, and everyday convenience—not to mention entertainment. Mobile apps and social media platforms help people stay connected with friends and loved ones, and information is right at a user's fingertips. If a person wants to look up a recipe, sell a piece of furniture, order a new book, make an appointment, or video chat with friends, it can all be done instantaneously. Being a resident of the digital world is extremely convenient.

> "CONSIDER SOMEONE WHO SIGNS UP AND GETS ON SOCIAL MEDIA WHEN THEY ARE 13 YEARS OLD AND POSTS AROUND TEN TIMES PER DAY. BY THE TIME THEY ARE 20, THEY WILL HAVE MADE 25,550 POSTS IN SEVEN YEARS."[3]
>
> —*GINA M. BIEGEL, LICENSED MARRIAGE AND FAMILY THERAPIST, 2019*

DIGITAL STRESS

Despite the benefits, a technologically advanced, constantly connected world has its drawbacks, and one of them is digital stress. This is a type of stress that is caused by negative interactions in the digital world. These negative interactions can be between an individual and another individual or group online, such as when a person receives a hurtful or mean-spirited comment. These negative interactions can also be between an individual and technology itself, such as when a smartphone becomes perpetually distracting or overwhelming.

Digital stress today often stems from social media use. While the internet itself can be a stressful place, social media creates ample opportunities for negative social interactions and stressful situations, adding to the problem. Social media can make a person worry about getting left out of fun experiences or social circles. It can even cause users to think that other people are having more fun or living better lives, even if this isn't true. According to Twenge, "I think young people, especially, look at the so-called 'highlight reels' people post on social [media] and compare

HOW MUCH IS TOO MUCH?

Although experts agree that technology and social media can be overused, they have not come to a consensus on how much is "too much." Most researchers agree that the content and the context matter, as well as the balance between screen time and non-screen time. A carefree hour reading articles and chatting with friends on the internet every afternoon could be okay, but if it's hard to move away from the smartphone screen, and if homework and dinner get pushed aside in favor of mindless scrolling, that could be a problem. Many professionals say screen time becomes too much when it interferes with mental health, relationships, and ambitions. According to Cal Newport, an associate professor of computer science at Georgetown University, "You want the feeling that your technology is improving your life, not detracting from its quality."[4]

SMARTPHONE SEPARATION ANXIETY

When separated from their mobile devices, such as smartphones and tablets, some people feel a sense of stress or panic. This feeling has become so common that researchers gave it a formal name—Smartphone Separation Anxiety, or *nomophobia*. According to a 2020 literature review on the subject, some users consider their mobile devices to be extensions of their bodies and important parts of their identities. The authors write, "Nomophobia promotes the development of mental disorders, personality disorders, as well as problems in people's self-esteem, loneliness, and happiness, especially in the younger population."[6]

themselves, so they may feel depressed or negative emotions as a result."[5]

Overuse of technology can cause digital stress too. This might mean using a tablet for hours at a time every single day, or it might mean playing video games late into the night instead of eating meals or completing homework assignments. Digital stress can also come from the need to constantly check or post on social media. While social media addiction is not officially recognized as a psychological diagnosis, teens who compulsively check social media apps throughout the day may feel as though they are addicted to the sites and apps they use. When social media takes precedence over important things such as meals, school, and family time, it is probably having a negative impact on the user's life.

SIGNS AND SYMPTOMS

There is no formal or professional medical diagnosis for digital and social media stress. However, there are plenty of signs and symptoms that can show when a person might be experiencing stress. Some symptoms are physical, such as stomachaches, headaches, dizziness, muscle tension, grinding teeth, and body aches. Others are associated with emotions and psychological wellness.

"AS SMARTPHONES EVOKE MORE PERSONAL MEMORIES, USERS EXTEND MORE OF THEIR IDENTITY ONTO THEIR SMARTPHONES."[7]

—RESEARCHERS SEUNGHEE HAN, KI JOON KIM, AND JANG HYUN KIM

WHAT IS ANXIETY?

One common symptom of digital stress is heightened anxiety. According to the American Psychological Association, anxiety is "an emotion characterized by feelings of tension, worried thoughts, and physical changes like increased blood pressure."[8] Other physical symptoms can include headaches, dizziness, sweating, shortness of breath, and a pounding heartbeat.

When people are concerned that they may be suffering from anxiety, they should reach out to a parent, teacher, counselor, or other trusted adult.

A headache is a common physical symptom of stress.

Feelings of anxiety, panic attacks, anger, and family conflict are all potential signs of stress.

Changes in behavior can also be linked to digital and social media stress. For example, someone suffering from this type of stress might exhibit increased secrecy, social isolation or withdrawal, and poorer grades in school. Additionally, sleep problems have been linked to screen time and mobile phone use. A 2019 study published in the International Journal of Environmental Research and Public Health stated, "Our results suggest a detrimental effect of screen time and mobile phone-related awakenings on sleep problems and related health symptoms."[9] Sleep deprivation and sleep disturbance are common signs of digital stress.

ARE THERE ANY SOLUTIONS?

The signs and symptoms of digital stress can have a severe negative impact on life. The good news is that digital and social media stress does not have to become a constant companion,

GAMING DISORDER

Researchers have studied the causes and symptoms of digital and social media stress, but there is still more to be done. While no formal diagnosis of digital stress exists, there is one related condition that has been formally classified as a disorder. In 2018, the World Health Organization (WHO) established gaming disorder as a mental health diagnosis in the International Classification of Diseases. This classification helps doctors and other professionals better identify and care for patients who may be experiencing the negative effects of excessive video game play. The American Psychiatric Association has not added gaming disorder to its *Diagnostic and Statistical Manual of Mental Disorders*, but it has recommended that the condition be researched further and considered for inclusion in the manual.

even for people who frequently use technology. There are plenty of ways to balance the digital world and the real world. Those might include learning how to reduce dependency on devices or even going tech free for a while. It can take time to set healthy boundaries and learn positive coping skills, but with hard work and persistence, it is possible to overcome digital and social media stress.

Social media and the digital world can lead to unique challenges and stressors, but it is possible to have a healthy, balanced relationship with technology.

It took several decades of innovation to develop the technology used today.

CHAPTER THREE

SOCIAL MEDIA HISTORY

Social media and digital tools are ubiquitous parts of most people's daily lives. It feels natural to connect with friends over video, interact with strangers via direct message, and leave comments on family members' pictures. But it wasn't always like this.

For most of modern history, social interactions were restricted to spending time together in person, writing letters, and eventually talking on landline telephones. The first cell phone—which weighed a whopping 2.5 pounds (1.1 kg)—was invented in 1973. Technology has changed rapidly in a matter of decades. Computers that could only do basic math evolved into watches that can search the internet. Though the history of modern technology might seem like a blip on the long arc of human history, the connected digital world was not invented overnight. The histories of cell phones, computers, and the internet are vital to understanding how humans went from writing letters to filming 60-second videos for social media.

THE FIRST SOCIAL MEDIA?

Some scholars cite the invention of the telegraph as the initial step toward today's social media. Before the telegraph, messages could only be sent via letters or human messengers. The telegraph was the first machine that could instantly send messages over a considerable distance. The machine used a code, invented by Samuel Morse, that assigned dots and dashes to each letter of the alphabet. Those dots and dashes were used for more than just emergency messages. The machine created, in effect, the first chat room for operators, as they tapped back and forth and joined each other's conversations. There were early forms of shorthand, much like today's "LOL." Operators used "GM" to say "Good morning" and "SFD" for "Stop for dinner." Telegraph operators became friends and even played games with each other, dictating moves in checkers or chess over the telegraph.

CELL PHONES

The first handheld cell phone prototype, launched by Motorola in 1973, was vastly different from the sleek, feature-rich devices that many people own today. It was clunky, heavy, and expensive, and a user could talk on the device for just 35 minutes after charging for ten hours. It would be another ten years before the company would introduce a commercial version of the product. In 1989, Motorola introduced the first flip phone, a cell phone that flipped closed, that was truly portable and attractive to consumers.

The cell phones of the 1980s and 1990s were used primarily as communication tools. People could use them to make calls and not much else. A few high-priced models had the ability to send emails. Limited as they were, these early cell phones grew popular. More and more consumers purchased them, and the technology continued to improve. In December 1992, a computer programmer in the United Kingdom sent the first text message. It said "Merry Christmas."[1]

COMPUTERS

As companies improved cell phone technology in the 1970s and 1980s, another revolution was underway in the computer industry. The history of computers dates back to the 1940s, when machines were built to perform complicated calculations. These early computers were huge, taking up entire

SOCIAL MEDIA USE BY AGE

When the first social media sites appeared, young adults were some of the first to start using them. Over the years, however, use by adults, and even by older adults, has seen a marked increase. According to the Pew Research Center, in 2005, 7 percent of 18- to 29-year-olds used at least one social media site, compared to 6 percent of 30- to 49-year-olds, 4 percent of 50- to 64-year-olds, and just 3 percent of those older than 65. In 2019, 90 percent of young adults reported using at least one social media site, compared to 82 percent of 30- to 49-year-olds, 69 percent of 50- to 64-year-olds, and 40 percent of those over 65.[2]

Apple CEO Steve Jobs unveiled the iMac in 1998. This computer was commonly used in homes and schools.

rooms. Throughout the 1950s, engineers worked to design computers that were smaller and capable of completing more advanced calculations. Computers that are similar to those in use today have been around since the 1960s. At the time they were mainly used in universities and office environments. It wasn't until the 1970s that computers were small and inexpensive enough to be used in homes.

Personal computers quickly gained popularity, especially among businesses. Some individuals and families bought these early computers for their homes, but there weren't many tasks people could do on them besides crunch data and type words.

Throughout the 1980s, companies such as IBM, Apple, and Compaq began to work aggressively in the personal computer space. Computer mice became commonplace, and floppy disks were used to save and transfer information. These upgrades, along with more affordable prices, made it easier for families to buy personal computers for the home during the 1990s. At the same time, schools across the United States adopted computers for use in classrooms. By the end of the millennium, desktop computers were a common sight in the American household.

THE INTERNET

It might feel as though the internet has always existed. In reality, it is only a few decades old. Its origins can be traced back to the Telex messaging network, a 1930s invention that connected printers to telephone lines, creating a system to distribute military messages. In 1949, the first modem gave computers the ability to communicate with each other over phone lines, and in 1958, engineers at IBM built a cross-country computer network for the US military.

In 1969, the US government's Advanced Research Projects Agency Network (ARPANET) became the first large-scale computer network to connect different kinds of computers together. Other networks followed. These early networks were used primarily in higher education and military settings. Though they had wide reaches within their communities, the networks were unable to link together. In order to make this happen, there would need to be a network for the networks—an *internet*.

Small networks continued to emerge throughout the 1970s and 1980s. In the mid-1980s, five supercomputer centers at major universities linked together to form the National Science Foundation Network (NSFNET). US military groups had their own network, MILNET. At the same time, the US government introduced a "network of networks" called the internet. By 1989, the internet—then a closed, noncommercial network, mostly used by tech enthusiasts—had gained 100,000 host computers and plenty of fans who were eager to create software and hardware to support it.[3]

One of those fans was Tim Berners-Lee. An English programmer and physicist, Berners-Lee pioneered facets of the internet that are still in use today, such as URLs, HTML, and the browser. He created the World Wide Web, which allowed users to author and organize information on the internet using pages that could be connected by

Sir Tim Berners-Lee was knighted in 2004 by the United Kingdom's Queen Elizabeth II for creating the World Wide Web.

links. Thanks to early volunteers who adapted the World Wide Web to various machines, as well as investors who became interested in the commercial possibilities of the web, it took off. By 2020, about 4.57 billion people, or 59 percent of the global population, were active internet users.[4] China, India, and the United States have the largest digital populations, or the highest number of internet users. In 2019, Berners-Lee reflected on his creation, writing, "While the web has created opportunity, given marginalised groups a voice, and made our daily lives easier, it has also created opportunity for scammers, given a voice to those who spread hatred, and made all kinds of crime easier to commit."[5]

"SINCE I GOT AN iPHONE, I HAVE SPENT MORE TIME ON MY PHONE BECAUSE OF SOCIAL MEDIA APPS. I CAUGHT MYSELF ON MULTIPLE OCCASIONS TELLING MYSELF 'ONLY 15 MORE MINUTES AND THEN I'LL START MY HOMEWORK,' BUT THEN I END UP SPENDING 30 MINUTES ON MY PHONE."[7]

—ALLISON CIERO, THE NEW YORK TIMES, 2020

SOCIAL MEDIA

In April 2020, researchers found that 3.8 billion people around the world were active social media users. That's almost half of the entire world population. Approximately 99 percent of those users accessed social media via mobile devices.[6]

The rise of social media is a recent development. Social media sites can be traced to the late 1990s, when users began maintaining weblogs, which are websites on which a user can regularly post writing, photos, or other content. These became known as *blogs*. Services such as LiveJournal and Blogger hosted blogs for free, so users did not need to pay for their own websites. The popularity of blogs exploded. On these blogs, individuals wrote about a variety of topics, from politics to parenting.

Blogging was one of the first ways that internet users learned to be social online. Message boards were another. Though their use can be traced back to the closed computer networks of the late 1970s, online message boards became popular in the 1990s. On message boards, users could chat anonymously and form communities around specific interests.

The late 1990s and early 2000s saw the rise of social networking sites. On these websites, users not only shared personal content (as they did on blogs) and connected with others (as they did on message boards), but they could seek out and connect with specific individuals. On some of the first social networking sites, such as Six Degrees, Friendster, LinkedIn, and Myspace, users could connect with friends, colleagues, and peers. Some sites were more popular than others. According to

SIX DEGREES

Myspace, launched in 2003, and Facebook, launched in 2004, were popular early social networking sites, but they weren't the first. That honor goes to Six Degrees, a site founded by Andrew Weinreich. Launched in 1997, the site included personal profiles, friends lists, and school affiliations. Users could send messages and invite contacts to join the site. The name of the site played on the idea of "six degrees of separation." This is the theory that all people are six or fewer social connections (or "degrees") away from one another. At its peak, Six Degrees had about 3.5 million registered users.[8] It was officially shut down in 2001.

SOCIAL GAMES

First introduced in the early 2000s, social games such as Farmville and Words With Friends quickly rose in popularity. These games asked users to invite their friends and acquaintances into game play. Unlike traditional video games, which are more immersive, social games encourage users to check in for shorter periods throughout the day. They also incentivize users to add friends, send messages, and post about these games online.

While these games can be casual and enjoyable, they've also been known to cause stress and annoyance to those who don't want to play. It's easy to become hooked on the games and feel the need to check in with them constantly. Some critics find the monetization of the games to be their worst fault. Many offer the option to spend real money in order to acquire points, items, or other incentives. Put together, the money and time users spend on social games can add up.

Lori Kozlowski, a writer at *Forbes*, "From 2005 to 2008, Myspace was the most visited social networking site in the world, often surpassing Google in number of visitors."[9]

As mobile phone use and popularity exploded in the mid-2000s, so did social media websites. Facebook and Gmail arrived in 2004, YouTube broke onto the scene in 2005, and Twitter was born in 2006. After that, sites such as Tumblr, Pinterest, WhatsApp, Ping, and Foursquare all filled their own niches in the social media sphere. People were suddenly able to share photos, links, music, and even their locations with friends, family members, and strangers online.

SMARTPHONES AND APPS

The first social media sites were only accessible via computers. Internet-connected smartphone technology didn't appear until the mid-2000s. Companies had released smartphones before 2007, but these devices were often difficult to use, and few people bought them. The phone industry changed in 2007 when Apple introduced the iPhone. In the speech he gave at the launch, Apple CEO Steve Jobs said, "Today, we're introducing three revolutionary products. The first one is a widescreen iPod with touch controls. The second is a revolutionary mobile phone. And the third is a breakthrough internet communications device."[10] Jobs then revealed that these three products were all one device: the iPhone.

Instead of a physical keyboard, this device had one big touch screen. Users could make calls, send text messages, browse the web, check email, listen to music, and make videos. Over time, Apple added the ability to download and access applications, which

"OUR WHOLE ROLE IN LIFE IS TO GIVE YOU SOMETHING YOU DIDN'T KNOW YOU WANTED. AND THEN ONCE YOU GET IT, YOU CAN'T IMAGINE YOUR LIFE WITHOUT IT. . . . AND YOU CAN COUNT ON APPLE DOING THAT."[11]

—APPLE CEO TIM COOK, 2012

allowed the phone to do even more. Suddenly, people were able to use social media apps from anywhere in the world, at any time.

Some of the most popular social media sites were born out of the smartphone boom. When smartphones introduced front-facing cameras, the selfie became commonplace. Paired with easy-to-use photo filters, it became easy for people to edit and upload photos to social media apps. Apps such as Snapchat, Instagram, WeChat, and TikTok take advantage of a smartphone's click-and-post capabilities, allowing users to document their lives in real time.

From the very first cell phones to the dawn of the internet age and beyond, people around the world have

HASHTAGS

The hashtag (#) is arguably one of the most useful tools to come out of social media's evolution. It was first used in the summer of 2007 by an early adopter of Twitter, Chris Messina, who thought it could be a helpful way to organize tweets on the platform. Combining the symbol with a keyword would make tweets about a particular subject easily searchable.

A few weeks later, Twitter used the hashtag #SanDiegoFire to organize conversations about California wildfires. Twitter fully embraced the hashtag in 2009. The hashtag was later adopted outside of Twitter. The symbol has been used to promote ideas, to market brands, and to create awareness. Some of the most notable hashtags of the 2010s were #BlackLivesMatter, #MeToo, and #MarchforOurLives.

Snapchat and other social media sites have filters that can be used over photos. These filters can distort the picture or enhance facial features.

harnessed technology and become more connected than ever before. Taken together, the history of technology and social media is a story of opportunity. Smartphones and lightning-fast internet connections help people build all kinds of relationships online. Of course, the last half century of progress has also produced a world in which social media and technology are a constant presence. The inescapable nature of social media adds to its potential to cause stress and distress in users' lives.

Tablets and other digital devices are increasingly being used in the classroom.

CHAPTER FOUR

YOUTH, YOUNG ADULTS, AND DIGITAL STRESS

Individuals born in the early 1990s, part of the generation commonly known as millennials, often got their first cell phones in middle or high school. Smartphones weren't available until they went to college. Those born between the late 1990s and early 2010s, known as Generation Z, grew up with smartphones and social networks. Because of this, they are called digital natives. They have been swiping touch screens and downloading apps from a young age. What's more, today's students are often required to use digital tools such as tablets, computers, smart boards, and even smartphones at school, and homework is often completed on a computer or other screen. Many teens cannot remember a time before the internet, which puts them in a privileged position when it comes to job skills, avenues of communication, and access to information. However, this blessing might also be considered a curse.

GENERATIONS

People are often divided into generations based on age groups. These divisions often emphasize common experiences shared by members of the same generation. There are several widely recognized names for these groups. The Silent Generation refers to those born between the late 1920s and mid-1940s. Baby Boomers were born from then to the mid-1960s. Generation X came after, born from that time until around 1980, and millennials were born from then to the mid-1990s. Generation Z includes those born from the mid-1990s onward. Those born in each generation have unique experiences with the digital world, which can lead to varying amounts of digital stress.

While people of all ages use digital tools, teenagers are online the most, and they tend to be the heaviest users of social media. Some people see their phones as extensions of their personalities. As professor Michael Patrick Lynch wrote for the *Guardian*, "Whether or not we actually *are* our phones, we increasingly identify with them. We increasingly see them and the digital life we lead on them as partly constituting who we psychologically are."[1]

When use of the internet and social media is a daily or even a constant occurrence, there are more opportunities for stress and negative outcomes. But frequent use isn't the only reason why teens are susceptible to digital and social media stress. Some of the main causes lie in their busy, stressful schedules—and in their brains.

STRESSED OUT

The story around digital and social media stress might be different if teens' lives weren't already so stressful. The life of a teenager is a busy one, as teens face plenty of academic and social pressures at school, and many are involved in jobs and countless activities. Teens also face uncertain futures. The cost of a college education continues to rise, and the job market remains competitive. Climate change, gun violence, poverty, and other major national and global issues add even more stress. Even without the unique pressures caused by the internet and social media, being a teen is stressful.

"I REALIZE THAT RESTRICTING TECHNOLOGY MIGHT BE AN UNREALISTIC DEMAND TO IMPOSE ON A GENERATION OF KIDS SO ACCUSTOMED TO BEING WIRED AT ALL TIMES. MY THREE DAUGHTERS WERE BORN IN 2006, 2009, AND 2012. . . . I HAVE ALREADY WITNESSED FIRSTHAND JUST HOW INGRAINED NEW MEDIA ARE IN THEIR YOUNG LIVES. I'VE OBSERVED MY TODDLER, BARELY OLD ENOUGH TO WALK, CONFIDENTLY SWIPING HER WAY THROUGH AN iPAD."[2]

—*JEAN TWENGE,*
THE ATLANTIC, 2017

A stressful life can cause people to feel frazzled, overwhelmed, strained, and even physically dizzy.

MEDIA MULTITASKING

Texting during class, scrolling through Instagram while watching a movie, or watching TikToks while editing a YouTube video are all examples of media multitasking. American teens spend about 29 percent of their screen time juggling multiple devices.[4] This might be a smartphone and a television, a tablet and a gaming console, or any other combination. When people multitask in this way, their brains work hard. But that doesn't mean their brains get stronger. Some studies have shown that media multitasking at a young age, when the brain is still developing, can result in poorer memory, increased impulsivity, and negative academic outcomes. Heavy media multitasking can also have an effect on a person's attention span. According to a 2018 report, "Heavier media multitaskers are more likely to suffer lapses of attention (among other attention-related differences) relative to lighter media multitaskers."[5]

Stress can also have short- and long-term impacts on people's brains and bodies. Researchers at Harvard Medical School found in 2018 that stress can interfere with cognition, memory, and attention. According to Jill Goldstein, a professor of psychiatry and medicine at Harvard, "Stress affects not only memory and many other brain functions, like mood and anxiety, but also promotes inflammation, which adversely affects heart health."[3] Goldstein also notes that the effects of stress can look different in various stages of life. Certain hormones, such as those secreted during puberty, can play a part in how stress affects an individual.

EFFECTS OF CHRONIC STRESS

In a 2017 article in the journal *Chronic Stress*, researchers outlined effects of chronic stress on the adolescent brain. The researchers found that adolescence is a particularly vulnerable period when it comes to stress, as the brain is changing at a rapid pace. According to the researchers, "There is a strong association between chronic stress and psychopathology in adolescence, with stress linked to depression, anxiety, and other internalizing and externalizing problems."[6] Some people might attribute the stress of adolescence to the pressures of schoolwork and extracurriculars, but there is evidence suggesting that social interactions, as well as interactions on social media, play a role. According to an article that appeared in *Nature Communications*, there are important connections between teens' social experiences, both online and off-line, and brain development. In particular, a teenager's brain can be especially sensitive

"I THINK THAT IN SOME WAYS IT COULD BE GOOD FOR ADULTS TO MONITOR HOW MUCH CHILDREN ARE ON THEIR PHONES TODAY. HOWEVER, WHO IS GOING TO MONITOR THE ADULTS?"[7]

—KAYLEE PHILLIPS, THE NEW YORK TIMES, 2020

to online acceptance or rejection, peer influence, and emotional interactions in media environments. The study's authors noted:

TELEVISION TIME

When it comes to statistics around digital media, it can seem like every figure keeps going up, as rates of smartphone ownership, hours spent online, and other indicators grow almost every year. But one number is trending downward: the amount of time tweens and teens spend watching television on a TV set. According to a 2019 study, only 33 percent of teens reported that they greatly enjoyed watching TV, which is a 12 percent drop from 2015, when participants were asked the same question. Of the TV they do watch, most of it is time-shifted rather than viewed live. This means watching recorded programs on a digital video recorder (DVR) or streaming them using a service such as Netflix or Hulu. On average, teens spend just 25 minutes a day watching television live.[9] As subscription services and mobile devices gain popularity, researchers don't expect that figure to get bigger.

There is evidence that the density of grey matter volume in the amygdala, a structure associated with emotional processing, is related to larger offline social networks, as well as larger online social networks. This suggests an important interplay between actual social experiences, both offline and online, and brain development.[8]

This means that social influences and media

The pressures of social media are a new challenge that today's teens face. More research is needed to understand the short- and long-term effects of digital stress.

use can have a significant effect on the developing adolescent brain.

Though there is room for more research, the stressors of adolescence, including the pressures of social media and the digital world, can have harmful effects on teens' brains and bodies. At a time in life when teens are forming their identities and learning what it means to be a social being, the added layers of digital and social media stress are particularly unwelcome.

Social media gives teens more avenues for conversation with their peers. It also expands a person's social circle.

CHAPTER FIVE

SOCIAL MEDIA STRESS

During adolescence, it can feel as though stress is closing in from all angles. The combined pressures of school, social life, family dynamics, work, college applications, and other stressors can be overwhelming. Social media has a unique way of taking all of this stress and pressure and amplifying it to new heights.

When users post on social media, they aren't just posting for themselves. The wide social circle and the constant updates of social media can cause teens to make more social comparisons than they would otherwise. As people scroll through news feeds and click through stories, they get an up close and personal look at what everyone else is doing. It can become easy to compare themselves to the images and updates on social media. However, this presents a false reality. On social media, people usually don't show off the negative sides of life—the disappointments, the bad grades, the frustrations and fights. Instead, users are presented with highlight reels and selfies that have been edited to look ideal.

While these can be enjoyable to look at and engage with, they do not represent real life.

> "THERE'S LITTLE DIFFERENCE BETWEEN DETERMINEDLY SELF-PROMOTING ONLINE CELEBRITIES, AND THOSE OF US WHO SIMPLY GLOW WHEN OUR FACEBOOK POSTS OR INSTA POSTS GET A FEW MORE LIKES THAN USUAL: THE SCALE OF OUR AMBITIONS MIGHT BE DIFFERENT, BUT THE CRAVING FOR ATTENTION IS THE SAME."[1]
>
> —ALEXANDRA SAMUEL, PHD, TECHNOLOGY WRITER AND DATA JOURNALIST, 2019

INTERNET FAME

Thanks to social media, more people are famous than ever before, and many of today's celebrities reached that status in an extremely short amount of time. These days, it isn't just Hollywood actors and best-selling pop singers who receive public exposure—it's everyone. The possibility of gaining fame via TikTok, Instagram, YouTube, or other social media platforms is enticing, especially since the top social media celebrities can get paid very well for their content.

One term that has been born of the social media age is *influencer*. Social media influencers build knowledge, authority, and relationships that allow them to affect others' buying decisions. Influencers help sell products, and they also sell the idea of what is cool, fashionable, fun, attractive, and valuable. It can take time to become an influencer. For example, someone might start a YouTube channel about makeup. The YouTuber uses a variety of products to showcase his or her makeup skills through fun videos. Over time, by gaining enough viewers, that YouTuber could be contacted by makeup companies that will give free products or money in exchange for promoting those products in videos. The presence of a sponsored product transforms a video from an inside look into a YouTuber's

FILTERS

Photo filters have become a hugely popular part of social media. Some of the most basic filters can alter lighting and colors, while more advanced filters can add accessories, change bone structure, and even erase pimples. But the act of applying filters can lead to self-scrutiny and what some are calling "Snapchat dysmorphia" or "selfie dysmorphia." This name comes from a mental health disorder called body dysmorphia. According to the Mayo Clinic, a top US hospital, body dysmorphia is a condition "in which you can't stop thinking about one or more perceived defects or flaws in your appearance—a flaw that appears minor or can't be seen by others."[2]

Most people already compare themselves to others. But the world of filters makes those comparisons even more unrealistic and sometimes damaging. When people get used to seeing airbrushed images of themselves, it can be daunting or even impossible to look at their own faces in the mirror.

Beauty influencers on social media might be sponsored by brands to promote certain products to their followers.

regular makeup routine to a personalized commercial for the makeup company.

It can be confusing to navigate a world of social media influencers or celebrities and "regular" social media users. Everyone has different intentions and motivations. Is an Instagrammer promoting a new brand of soap because she is getting paid by the brand, or because she truly thinks it is a superior product? Is a company sending free samples as a gift or as an advertisement? The line between influencer and regular social media user can be a very thin one.

As it becomes easier to become famous on social media, more teens are feeling pressure to curate profiles that will get them noticed and help them gain followers. This is troubling for several reasons. First, the desire for fame can lead people to behave in ways they might not otherwise. A person may end up making decisions he regrets because of

FACTS AND FAKES

"Fake news" refers to outrageous and sometimes shocking headlines that are simply not true. On social media, links are shared so quickly and widely that it can be difficult to discern the difference between real facts and fake news stories. According to a 2020 survey from Common Sense Media, less than half of kids say that they know how to separate fake news stories from real ones.[3] Even if teens aren't sharing fake news online, it can add tension to relationships with family and friends. Researchers found that Americans older than 65 were those most likely to share misleading or fake news with their Facebook friends.[4] There is no quick fix that will eliminate fake news, but media literacy programs can help people of all ages separate credible content from falsehoods. As more schools implement such programs, advocates hope readers will feel more confident when it comes to navigating news.

the pressure to gain likes and followers. For example, in 2018, YouTube influencer Logan Paul uploaded a video of himself and his friends in Aokigahara, a Japanese forest known as the site of frequent suicides. In the video, which gained six million views, Paul was shown standing next to a corpse. Despite the popularity of the video, there was immense public outcry, and Paul lost several brand sponsors. In a written apology, Paul said, "I should have never posted the video. I should have put the cameras down and stopped recording what we were going through. There's a lot of things I should have done differently but I didn't."[5] Poor decisions or risky behavior can be captured and immortalized online, causing problems down the road.

Additionally, the race to get famous can negatively affect mental and emotional health. Seeing others rack up followers and likes can make a person feel inadequate. It's worth remembering that some social media influencers and brands are involved in the practice of purchasing followers. For as little as three dollars, an influencer can buy hundreds of followers from an online service.[6] These "ghost followers" aren't actual human beings. They are usually inactive accounts or "bots," which are accounts created specifically to drive up a person's follower count.

GETTING NOTIFIED

The constant buzz of a cell phone or the appearance of a notification on a screen can make a person feel as though there is always something to be checking, which is another contributor to feelings of anxiety and stress. In an article for the *New York Times* magazine, John Herrman offers a clear description of what makes mobile notifications, or "dots," so appealing. He writes:

What's so powerful about the dots is that until we investigate them, they could signify anything: a career-altering email; a reminder that Winter Sales End Soon; a match, a date, a "we need to talk." The same badge might lead to word that Grandma's in the hospital or that, according to a prerecorded voice, the home-security system you don't own

"I MOST DEFINITELY SEE THE CONNECTION BETWEEN HIGHER LEVELS OF STRESS AND BEING ON YOUR PHONE FOR A MORE THAN NEEDED AMOUNT OF TIME. SCROLLING THROUGH SOCIAL MEDIA AND LOOKING AT SMALL SQUARE SIZED SNAPSHOTS OF A PERSON'S 'PICTURE PERFECT LIFE' CAN REALLY HAVE AN EFFECT ON BOTH SELF-ESTEEM AND MENTAL HEALTH."[7]

—*SADIE DUNNE, THE NEW YORK TIMES, 2020*

THE PLUS SIDE

While social media can cause unique pressures and stress, it can also be a positive part of teens' lives. In a 2015 survey conducted by the Pew Research Center, 70 percent of teens reported that social platforms help them connect with their friends' feelings.[9] Sharing emotions and experiences on social media has the power to strengthen people's sense of empathy and their social awareness about various issues around their school, the country, and the world.

These platforms help build bridges between those who are different. At the same time, they can create important connections between those who are struggling with the same issues. Additionally, social media can offer a platform for teens to showcase their personalities and creativity, which can build confidence. Those who enjoy making art, playing music, and engaging in other creative pursuits can use social media to share their talents and connect with other creative individuals.

is in urgent need of attention or that, for the 51st time today, someone has posted in the group chat.[8]

As Herrman explains, there is an urgency to the notifications, even if what they are notifying people about is not urgent at all. When people post on social media apps or sites, they often feel the need to check in and see how many people have liked, commented on, or otherwise interacted with the post. Many teens want to be liked by their friends and peers, just like all people do, but this can extend into the digital world, causing teens to feel pressure to

People are often distracted by their phones after receiving
new notifications.

post content that others will like. Some teens feel the need
to only post content in which they are happy, having fun, or
doing something impressive or fashionable.

While most people spend time planning how they will
look or act in public, social media adds a new dimension.
Sometimes it even adds multiple dimensions, as teens
need to consider how they present themselves on various
apps and to different audiences. It is not easy to create one
simple, authentic digital persona. Sometimes the emotional
and social work that goes into creating a social media
presence can be its own source of stress and pressure.

In-person bullying and cyberbullying both can have lasting negative effects on a victim's mental health.

CHAPTER SIX

NEGATIVITY ONLINE

No one wants to experience digital stress. The pressures people experience online can have real-life consequences and can even cause physical symptoms, such as headaches, stomachaches, and sleep disruption. Social pressures and stress of any kind can be difficult to deal with, but some people use the internet and social media to intentionally harm others. Cyberbullying, public shaming, impersonation, and smothering are just a few examples of experiences that can not only cause stress but can have long-term negative consequences.

Young people who experience cyberbullying are at a greater risk than those who don't when it comes to self-harm and suicidal behaviors. A 2019 study of students in the United Kingdom linked cyberbullying with symptoms of post-traumatic stress (PTS) in victims. The researchers cautioned, "Parents, teachers, and health professionals need to be aware of possible PTS symptoms in young people involved in cyberbullying."[1] According to the Mayo Clinic, a top US hospital, common symptoms of PTS include negative mood changes, intrusive memories, and avoidance of situations that remind the victim of the traumatic situation.

PERSONAL ATTACKS AND HARASSMENT

Bullying has long been a problem in schools, but the online world set the stage for bullying beyond school walls. According to a 2019 study conducted by the Cyberbullying Research Center, about 37 percent of young people ages 12 to 17 say they have been bullied online. Around 30 percent say it has happened more than once.[2] Because the study relied on self-reported data, actual numbers could be higher or lower.

Someone who is being cyberbullied might receive mean messages or targeted comments, or she might see posts about herself that others have made. Many times, hateful messages are anonymous. A message of "You're ugly" or "I hate you" can be just as damaging whether it comes from

> "NAME-CALLING AND RUMOR-SPREADING HAVE LONG BEEN AN UNPLEASANT AND CHALLENGING ASPECT OF ADOLESCENT LIFE. BUT THE PROLIFERATION OF SMARTPHONES AND THE RISE OF SOCIAL MEDIA HAS TRANSFORMED WHERE, WHEN, AND HOW BULLYING TAKES PLACE."[3]
>
> —MONICA ANDERSON, ASSOCIATE DIRECTOR OF RESEARCH AT THE PEW RESEARCH CENTER, 2018

a stranger or from a known peer. A physical threat of violence can be terrifying no matter who sends it. Sometimes apps are designed to be anonymous, making it more difficult to take action against perpetrators.

These harassing behaviors can be specific to the social media platforms they happen on. For example, sub-tweeting is when someone writes a tweet about another person without using that person's username. Bullying, subtweeting, and offensive name-calling are common forms of online harassment.

SWATTING

Swatting is a form of online harassment that can be dangerous and even deadly. It involves calling 911 to generate an unnecessary emergency response to a person's house. The intent is to get a heavily armed special weapons and tactics (SWAT) team to enter someone's home, even though no crime has been committed. A troop of SWAT officers swarming a person's home is a terrifying experience—and it's potentially dangerous. In 2019, a man in Wichita, Kansas, was fatally shot by police when his home was swatted. He was not the swatter's intended target. The man who called in the fake report was sentenced to 20 years in prison.

An anonymous internet celebrity spoke to *Wired* about the dangers of swatting, saying, "Swatting truly is terrifying. . . . You can just be having a meal with your family and a SWAT team arrives, yelling, guns out. It's something that won't just affect you but also every living thing inside of your home."[4]

Social media can be used to target others. Cyberbullying and mean messages can come from someone the victim knows or from a stranger online.

HUMILIATION

Another popular form of online harassment is humiliation, which can take various forms. A bully might post an embarrassing photo of another person or share a screenshot from a conversation that was supposed to be private. Sometimes private messages intended for only one person suddenly go public, and then they are seen by an entire school or community. This can be incredibly humiliating, especially when explicit or private images are shared.

Sometimes people start false rumors or share false information in order to turn people against an individual. Impersonation—the act of pretending to be someone else—can be particularly damaging and difficult to resolve. Bullies can create fake social media accounts online or hack others' real accounts, and then they impersonate those people in embarrassing ways. It may take weeks or even months for the victims to get all of their social media accounts in order again. Damage to their reputations may be permanent.

> "INSTAGRAM IS MANY TEENS' ENTIRE SOCIAL INFRASTRUCTURE; AT ITS MOST DESTRUCTIVE, BULLYING SOMEONE ON THERE IS THE DIGITAL EQUIVALENT OF TAPING MEAN FLYERS ALL OVER SOMEONE'S SCHOOL, AND HER HOME, AND HER FRIENDS' HOMES."[5]
>
> —TAYLOR LORENZ, THE ATLANTIC, 2018

STALKING AND SMOTHERING

While many negative interactions online stem from cyberbullies or others with malicious intent, some come from those who seem to be kind or loving. Smothering occurs when a person contacts someone excessively.

HARASSMENT AND GENDER

According to data compiled by the Pew Research Center in 2018, teen girls and teen boys are equally likely to experience cyberbullying, but there are some differences when it comes to the types of harassment they encounter online. Approximately 39 percent of girls surveyed said someone has spread false rumors about them online, compared with 26 percent of boys. Additionally, about 29 percent of girls said they were the recipient of explicit images they did not ask for. Only 20 percent of boys said the same. When it came to other types of harassment, such as physical threats and offensive name-calling, boys and girls were almost equally likely to experience them.[6]

This might include sending photos the person did not ask for, or it may involve bombarding someone with messages and comments on all of her social media accounts. Excessive texting can also be a type of smothering. This can cause a person to feel overwhelmed and stressed, especially if she has expressed that she does not want to receive the messages or continue the relationship.

Smothering is closely tied to social pressure. While someone could be smothered by a stranger online, this type of behavior typically occurs within a relationship. This could be a relationship between family members, friends, or significant others. When someone is feeling smothered, he might feel pressured to comply with requests for access to online accounts. Someone who asks another person to share his password, show her all of his text messages, or give her access to his social media accounts could be exhibiting smothering or even stalking behavior. Some people may go as far as breaking into another person's accounts or devices or accessing phone, computer, or social media accounts without permission.

On the extreme end of smothering is stalking. Licensed clinic social worker Jessica Klein says, "We define stalking as unwanted or obsessive behavior toward an individual intended to frighten or coerce. This can include bombarding the individual with texts, emails, phone calls or gifts, showing up at someone's house or workplace, explicit or implicit threats, blackmail,

CATFISHING

The term *catfishing* was coined in 2010, thanks to a documentary about a person who lied about her identity online. Catfishing is the act of creating a fake identity or social media presence online, usually in order to target a specific victim. People who do this may want to harm others, or steal from them. Sometimes people catfish to gain attention, acclaim, romance, or money.

No matter the motivation behind their creation, fake online identities can be dangerous. It's wise to look out for signs of catfishing when meeting people online, especially on dating websites and apps. A few common signs of catfishers are few followers, lack of photo tags, and not wanting to make video calls.

DIGITAL SELF-HARM

Emotional highs and lows are common during adolescence. For some teenagers, those emotions take the form of feelings of anxiety and depression. To cope with their pain, about 13 to 18 percent of distressed teens physically injure themselves. While self-harm has long been an issue for teenagers, some are turning toward a new form called digital self-harm. Teens who engage in digital self-harm post mean and derogatory comments about themselves online. Some cyberbully themselves through ghost accounts.

One 2016 study published in the *Adolescent Journal of Health* showed that 6 percent of surveyed youth engaged in some form of digital self-harm. Child psychologist Sheryl Gonzalez Ziegler said, "Similar to teens who self-harm by cutting, kids who cyberbully themselves often suffer silently, feeling like they don't have a friend or adult to confide in."[8] When it comes to any type of self-harm, digital or otherwise, a nonjudgmental listener can be an important lifeline.

or even sexual assault."[7] Some people are stalked by a person they know, such as a partner, friend, or acquaintance. This person might constantly ask them where they are, what they are doing, or who they are with, with no regard for the individual's privacy. Stalkers also target strangers. They may try to track down a person's address or phone number or send messages incessantly. Of using social media to stalk someone, also known as "cyberstalking," Klein says, "Social media is a tool, like anything else. You can use it to keep tabs on your friends, but you can also use it to make someone's life miserable."[9]

FIGHTING DIGITAL HARASSMENT

If a person is experiencing smothering, stalking, hacking, digital impersonation, or cyberbullying in any of its forms, it's important to act quickly by telling someone. Talking to a parent, teacher, coach, therapist, or other trusted adult can provide victims with the support they need to stop the harassment. Some online behaviors, such as impersonation, stalking, and cyberbullying, are against the law in certain scenarios and can lead to legal consequences. If necessary, a trusted adult can also help mediate the situation or figure out when it is the right time to contact internet service providers, website moderators, social media

WAIT UNTIL 8TH

Many experts are concerned about the stress caused by social media and devices such as smartphones. One initiative, Wait Until 8th, is aiming to delay kids' smartphone use. The initiative asks parents to pledge that they won't provide a smartphone to their kids until at least eighth grade, providing them with only basic phones until then. That way kids can avoid the dangers and distractions of smartphones and focus on being kids. The hope is that if many parents follow this advice, families will feel less pressure to give smartphones to their young children.

platforms, or law enforcement. According to the National Crime Prevention Council (NCPC), only one in ten teen victims of cyberbullying tells a parent or trusted adult about the abuse.[10] But telling someone is an important step when it comes to ending cyberbullying. It can also be helpful to keep a record of the bullying. Screenshots are one of the best ways to report an instance of cyberbullying, especially if the bully deletes her or his comments. The NCPC suggests that teens block a cyberbully's messages, keep a record of incidents through screenshots or printed copies, and remember to never seek revenge on a cyberbully. When it comes to cyberbullying and digital harassment, experts say retaliation is never the answer. Negative online behavior is something that a person engages in. Online behavior does not define who a person is— and with time and intention, it can be changed.

Someone who is experiencing cyberbullying or other harassing online behaviors should speak to a trusted adult about how to address the situation.

Research shows that multitasking lowers concentration and makes it more difficult to complete tasks such as studying.

CHAPTER SEVEN

DISTRACTION, ADDICTION, AND EMOTIONAL CONSEQUENCES

Social media and the online world can affect emotions, relationships, and day-to-day life, but some experts take it a step further, believing that the digital realm can also adversely affect brain development, memory, learning, and focus. These experts study internet users for whom social media has become an extreme distraction, replacing important obligations such as work and school, as well as those for whom social media has become a dangerous addiction, consuming almost all of their waking hours. Though research on these issues is still in its early stages, all signs point to screens and social media as major sources of distraction and addiction.

DISTRACTION

When it comes to social media and the internet, there's no getting around the fact that many people are constantly connected. As smart watches and other wearables have become more popular, some people are literally connected to their devices at all times. This can be convenient, especially when it's time to order takeout or ask a question of a digital assistant. But it can also amplify the problems with these devices.

All of the different forms of social media and digital media can lead users to multitask. One study showed that high percentages of teens watched TV, used social media, and texted while doing homework. Most of the teens did not believe that their multitasking lowered the quality of their work. However, research has shown that multitasking decreases productivity. It takes time to reorient the brain when transitioning between activities. This can slow down work. Additionally, studies show that multitasking makes it harder for the brain to create memories that can be accurately retrieved in the future, which means that multitasking while studying might not be the smartest way to prepare for a big test.

When thinking about distraction, it is also worth considering the toll it takes on other areas of life. Devices can distract people from conversations with friends and

Being distracted while driving can have serious consequences to drivers and passengers.

family, which hurts relationships. Devices can also distract people from doing things they love. The more time they spend checking social media and scrolling through apps, the less time they spend on hobbies and passions such as sports, music, books, and nature.

Additionally, devices can be dangerous when they're used at the wrong times, such as while driving or bicycling. ScienceDaily reports, "More than a quarter of car accidents reported each year are attributed to some form of distraction among drivers, often the result of talking or texting while driving. Nine people are estimated to die every day in the US from distracted driving and 330,000 injuries occur each year because of texting while driving, which is also the most common cause of death in teenagers."[1]

TAKING CHARGE

The prevalence of digital devices has led to a nationwide debate about the impact of screen time on young people. But it isn't just experts who are thinking and talking about this issue. Many are evaluating their own screen time and deciding how much is too much for them. According to a 2018 survey by the Pew Research Center, about 54 percent of US teens say they spend too much time on their cell phones, and 52 percent say they are taking steps to cut back on their phone use. Similarly, 57 percent say they have tried to limit their use of social media. It seems that teens are making these choices for a reason. Around 60 percent of surveyed teens said "spending too much time online" is a major problem for people their age.[2]

ADDICTION

It's easy to joke with friends and family about being "addicted" to devices. While people may spend many hours a day clicking and scrolling, for a small number of individuals, social media or internet addiction is a reality. This situation is considered a behavioral addiction, which is different from a physical addiction. A person with a physical addiction, such as an addiction to drugs, alcohol, or nicotine, has become physically dependent on a substance. If the person were to stop using the substance, they would experience physical withdrawal symptoms, such as tremors and fatigue. Someone with a behavioral addiction could be addicted to behaviors such as gambling, exercise, eating, or shopping. Pleasurable experiences cause the brain to release neurochemicals that are picked up by receptors in the brain and body. The chemicals make a person feel good and can even give a person the feeling

"THE NEGATIVE IMPACT OF SOCIAL MEDIA IS APPARENT WHETHER IT'S DEEMED CLINICAL ADDICTION OR NOT. MOST PEOPLE'S SOCIAL MEDIA USE IS HABITUAL ENOUGH THAT IT SPILLS OVER INTO OTHER AREAS OF THEIR LIVES. IT RESULTS IN BEHAVIOR THAT IS PROBLEMATIC AND DANGEROUS, SUCH AS CHECKING SOCIAL MEDIA WHILE DRIVING."[4]
—*MARK GRIFFITHS AND DARIA KUSS, THE WASHINGTON POST, 2018*

of a high. This is not necessarily a bad thing. The problem is when people begin to seek these highs too often, according to Hilarie Cash, PhD, a founding member of the reSTART program for internet and gaming addicts. "This is what we call tolerance, and we no longer get the high from the same level of activity or drug use," she says. "Now, we need more. And if we go without, we go into withdrawal."[3] People continue seeking the high of the behavior, engaging more and more until it takes over their lives.

When screen time begins interfering with time spent with family and friends, it can be a sign of behavioral addiction.

Those who are addicted to social media have an uncontrollable urge to check their social media apps and sites, and they devote so much time to social media that it detracts from other important areas of their life, such as sleeping, eating, work, and relationships. Social media is incredibly addictive, in part because of the ways in which social media platforms and apps affect people's brains. When a person sees a new notification on a social media platform, the reward center in the person's brain activates. Social media provides an endless stream of immediate rewards in the form of likes and comments. As the brain becomes accustomed to these rewards, it rewires itself, making users desire the rewards even more.

Those who are addicted to social media may even experience withdrawal symptoms when they try to pull away. These unpleasant emotional and psychological symptoms can make it extremely difficult to curb an addiction. Some common withdrawal symptoms include poor concentration, irritability, increased anxiety, and depression. When a user ignores real-life responsibilities, physical health, or in-person relationships in favor of the digital and social media realms, it becomes cause for concern.

EMOTIONAL AND SOCIAL CONSEQUENCES

Many researchers have found that overuse of social media can also have a detrimental effect on emotional and social health. Studies have shown that social media overuse may

FAMILY TENSION

When people are distracted by frequent technology and social media use, it doesn't just affect themselves. It can lead to conflicts within families—and young people aren't the only ones overusing their devices and becoming distracted. In one survey of children and parents, over half of the children felt that their parents checked their devices too often. Thirty-two percent of kids felt unimportant when their parents were distracted by their phones.[5]

> "DECADES OF RESEARCH ON HAPPINESS TELL US THAT ENGAGING POSITIVELY WITH OTHERS IS CRITICAL FOR OUR WELL-BEING. MODERN TECHNOLOGY MAY BE WONDERFUL, BUT IT CAN EASILY SIDETRACK US AND TAKE AWAY FROM THE SPECIAL MOMENTS WE HAVE WITH FRIENDS AND FAMILY IN PERSON."[6]
>
> —RYAN DWYER, RESEARCHER AND PhD CANDIDATE AT THE UNIVERSITY OF BRITISH COLUMBIA, 2018

actually lower a person's empathy. Time spent with media, even social media, detracts from face-to-face, in-person time with others. When people aren't conversing with and learning from other people, they miss the subtleties of facial expressions, gestures, laughter, tones, and other conversational cues. A lack of experience with vocal and visual cues can hinder an individual's ability to understand the emotions of others, create strong relationships, and accurately interpret what others are saying. There is still much research to be done into the effects of digital and social media on social-emotional health. Until more studies can be done, hard data remains limited, and researchers remain cautiously concerned.

Research also shows that overuse of social media can negatively affect a person's mental health, making the individual feel increasingly isolated or unhappy. On sites such as Instagram and Facebook, users see carefully curated versions of people's lives. Many of these posts, especially those posted by influencers, are specifically designed to appeal to social media users, and some are even targeted to specific demographics, such as teenage girls or youth athletes. While it is possible to feel inspired by people on the internet, they can also leave users feeling inadequate, self-conscious, jealous, dissatisfied, and even depressed. When those comparisons happen, a social media user can be left feeling completely uninspired, no matter the original intent of the poster.

BODY IMAGE

Image-based social media sites and apps such as Instagram and Facebook have become popular platforms for food and fitness posts. While these posts can provide useful knowledge, they can also invite users to examine their own eating habits, diets, and bodies through a negative lens. A 2016 study from the University of Pittsburgh found a correlation between eating disorders and time spent scrolling through social media apps and sites. Study participants who spent more time on social media had 2.2 times the risk of reporting eating and body image concerns compared to those who spent less time on social media. According to the authors of the study, "Research has shown that individuals tend to post images online that present themselves positively. Therefore, users are likely to select from hundreds of more 'accurate' photos the scant few which may make the subject appear thinner and more attractive, in line with current social ideals."[7]

The distracting, addictive, and emotionally harmful aspects of social media and the internet are enough to give experts and users pause. As more and more individuals have sought help for social media, gaming, and internet addictions, as well as depression and anxiety linked to digital media use, psychiatrists and treatment centers are stepping up to provide care. Though internet addiction and social media addiction are not officially classified as disorders, specialty treatment centers have opened across the United States, and existing centers have added services that help treat compulsive internet and social media behaviors. The Lindner Center of Hope in Ohio offers a "Reboot" program aimed at teens who are addicted to social media, online gaming, or the internet. These services can help young people overcome negative relationships with digital technology and help them reconnect to a healthier, happier life.

Social media users typically upload pictures of themselves at their best. It is important to remember that their posts do not show a complete picture of their lives.

Spending time outside with friends is one way to take a break from screens.

CHAPTER EIGHT

OVERCOMING DIGITAL AND SOCIAL MEDIA STRESS

When an individual is suffering from digital or social media stress, it can feel like there is no end in sight. New devices and apps are released every year, connecting users to a seemingly endless web of social media platforms. According to Dr. Shilagh Mirgain, a psychologist at the University of Wisconsin-Madison, "Technology has become so embedded in daily life it can be hard to imagine stepping away. But it's important to establish boundaries and take control. When we do, it will benefit our mental and physical health in so many ways."[1]

Luckily, there are coping mechanisms to reduce the amount of stress that comes from technology and social media. But that doesn't mean everyone needs to log out indefinitely. When it comes to curbing the negative effects of social media use, Anna Vannucci, research associate at Connecticut Children's Medical Center, suggests moderation. She says, "You don't have to take an all or nothing approach to detoxing a little bit from social media."[2] Moderation can be one positive step toward developing a healthier relationship with social media.

TRACK USAGE

"ROUGHLY FOUR-IN-TEN TEEN CELLPHONE USERS (43 PERCENT) SAY THEY OFTEN OR SOMETIMES USE THEIR PHONE TO AVOID INTERACTING WITH PEOPLE."[3]

—*PEW RESEARCH CENTER, 2019*

When stress of any type arises in a person's life, one of the first and most helpful things that person can do is locate the source of the stress. Time-tracking apps give users a clear picture of how they use their time online. With the app Screen Time, users can generate reports about how much time they spend on various apps and websites. Apple, Android, Google, and other companies have made Screen Time and similar apps available for their devices and operating systems. Many of these apps also allow users to set reminders and limit the amount of daily or weekly time they spend in various apps or app categories. This can be a helpful first step in an effort to limit the amount of social media stress in one's life. In addition to tracking, some programs can block distracting apps or websites. For example, a person could allow only one hour of time on social media sites per day, or only allow access to these sites at a certain time of day. Keeping track of time

Blocking or limiting certain apps can help someone concentrate on homework and other tasks without getting distracted.

spent online can help people prioritize the most important aspects of their online routines, such as keeping in touch with friends and family.

CLEAN THE FEED

After figuring out which apps and types of sites a person is spending the most time on and perhaps overusing, it might be time to "clean the feed." This means taking stock of the accounts being followed and removing any that are unnecessary or detrimental to mental health. Airen Petalbert, a writer for Tech Times, describes the importance of being intentional about which accounts a

UNFRIEND AND UNFOLLOW

It can be difficult to know when it is time to unfriend, unfollow, or even block someone on Facebook. All friendships and relationships have their ups and downs, and it might not always be necessary to unfriend a person who has differing opinions or interests. Unfollowing, unfriending, and blocking are similar actions, but the results are different, and they are useful in different situations. If a user wants to stop seeing a person's posts but does not want to completely stop interacting with that person's social media, the user can unfollow. This keeps the other person's posts from appearing in the user's feed. A more permanent solution is to unfriend. If a user unfriends another person, the person will not receive a notification. However, if the other person looks at her friends list, she will know she was unfriended. To completely cut contact, a user can block another person, meaning neither one can contact the other.

person follows. Petalbert says, "Here's a social media tip every user must know by heart: follow only the topics and people that are good for your mental health."[4] This might mean unfollowing accounts on Instagram or Twitter, especially those that cause feelings of self-consciousness, jealousy, or negativity. It might also mean unfriending people the user doesn't know or frequently contact. A friend list can be limited to just close friends. Many apps now offer options to stop seeing someone's posts without alerting the other person.

However, it is also important to note that unfollowing or unfriending to protect mental health does not necessarily mean avoiding pages or people who hold differing opinions and viewpoints, have different life experiences, or otherwise challenge the status quo. Social media is a key avenue for education and social change. On social media, people can interact with information, people, places, and ideas that they wouldn't otherwise seek out, especially if they intentionally follow a diverse array of people and organizations. While the social media accounts a person follows can and should be intellectually stimulating and challenging, they should not be emotionally painful, depressing, or abusive. When people are truly able to disconnect from those who negatively affect their mental health, cleaning up a news feed can go a long way toward both limiting the amount of time spent online and improving the quality of that time.

TURN DOWN THE VOLUME

For some people, the constant hum of the digital world can be an

"I DEFINITELY FEEL STRESS WITH ONLINE PROFILES, SOCIAL MEDIA, TO KEEP UP, MAINTAIN MY PROFILES AND STUFF. IT KIND OF WORRIES ME THAT I'M ON MY PHONE SO MUCH."[5]

—EMILY MOGAVERO, HIGH SCHOOL STUDENT IN BUFFALO, NEW YORK, 2019

REACH OUT

Sometimes digital and social media stress demands a stronger response than unfollowing or taking some time off-line. When a person feels threatened, unsafe, or depressed, it's time to get help by reaching out to people who care. Teens can reach out to a teacher, parent, sibling, counselor, boss, or another trusted adult. Whether the situation involves mediating with a bully or figuring out what to do in a catfishing scenario, it's important to be honest about digital struggles and let other people help.

immense distraction. There are notifications, emails, 24-hour news cycles, and so much more to contend with online. To deal with the distraction, clinical psychologist Jennifer Guttman, PsyD, suggests that people turn the ringtone, notification sounds, and vibration off on their phones. This can help create time in which the phone is not interrupting the flow of work, conversation, or thoughts. In addition to blocking these auditory cues, Guttman also suggests turning off visual notifications for applications. She writes, "Give yourself certain times during the day when you check your phone for messages and stick to those times. This gives you long breaks in between when you're off the phone."[6] Turning off notifications can help users build valuable space between themselves and overused apps without completely deleting the apps or logging out. Other experts suggest putting physical distance between the phone and the user.

Examples include placing the phone in a drawer or closet during homework time or not bringing a phone to the dinner table. Another common suggestion is to buy an alarm clock for nighttime use, rather than leave the phone on a bedside table. This can help reduce the amount of time spent scrolling through apps at night and first thing in the morning.

TAKE A DIGITAL BREAK

When social media and digital stress become too much to handle, it might be time to take a digital break or "detox." Blogger Jason Zook felt that his heavy social media use was having a detrimental effect on his life, so he took a 30-day social media break. Of his experience, he wrote, "One of my first realizations was just how much time can

GENERALIZED STRESS

When working to overcome digital stress, it's important to create boundaries around social media and the internet. But there are also simple things a person can do to help manage and reduce stress in general. Any form of exercise can reduce stress, whether it's walking, running, swimming, or playing other sports. Exercising outside can be extra beneficial, as spending time in green space has also been shown to help relieve stress. Mindfulness activities such as yoga, coloring, and meditation can help turn down the volume on stress, as can cutting out caffeinated drinks such as coffee, soda, and energy drinks. Of course, it can also be helpful to talk to someone, such as a counselor, teacher, parent, or friend.

BLUE LIGHT

Those who find themselves using screens for many hours each day might find that their eyes are dry and tired. One cause of that eye strain is the blue light emitted by digital screens, which is known to have an effect on a person's circadian rhythm, the biological clock inside a person that tells the person when it's time to be asleep.

Instead of cutting back on screen use, some people are adopting a new accessory: blue light–blocking glasses, which have special lenses that filter out the blue light given off by digital screens. According to manufacturers, these lenses can help reduce the negative effects of blue light. While these glasses have become popular with casual users and screen addicts alike, little research has been done into their effectiveness.

be wasted browsing social networks without knowing it. I could feel myself wanting to sneak a peek at Facebook."[7] As Zook experienced, it is incredibly difficult to quit social media cold turkey. In order to stay off of apps, people might need to delete them or deactivate their accounts. Someone could ask a trusted friend to change the account passwords. These steps can help people stay off-line, even when they feel the itch to log in.

WHAT'S NEXT?

When setting aside a phone, tablet, or computer, even for a short time, it's helpful to think about some activities that could take the place of the internet and social media. Instead of checking social media apps before falling

Limiting the time spent on mobile devices allows people to spend time on other hobbies.

asleep, a person can read a book or work on a craft. In the hours normally spent creating content or taking photos, a person could join a new club, play a sport, or spend time with friends. Users might also consider whether there is anything they have been avoiding. Is social media being used as a distraction from homework, instrument practice, chores, social time, or family time? Once the gadgets are put away, a person can face challenges head-on. People may be surprised at how much time is suddenly available after logging out, going off-line, or turning off devices.

As technology becomes a part of daily life, it is important to develop a healthy relationship with the digital world.

CHAPTER NINE

FINDING A BALANCE

While it is important to acknowledge the stress that social media and the digital world can bring to users' lives, this stress is not the end of the story, and the issue isn't always clear-cut. Adam Mosseri, the head of Instagram, said in a 2019 interview, "Technology is not inherently good, and it's not inherently bad. For those of us who work in the industry, it's our responsibility to magnify the good and address the bad as effectively as we can."[1] Within the world of cyberbullying, digital distraction, negative mental health outcomes, and social media addiction, there is still room for growth, and there are plenty of opportunities on the horizon. As more people understand these issues, community members, tech companies, politicians, families, and others can come together to make the digital world a more positive place. It is easy to assume that the battle against digital and social media stress is hopeless. But there are plenty of reasons to have hope.

AWAY FOR THE DAY

One movement that is gaining traction in schools is called Away for the Day. According to research, teens are more socially and academically engaged when their phones are away during school hours. Away for the Day asks parents, teachers, and school leaders to work toward instituting policies in which phones are kept in lockers or left at home during the school day. These policies would guarantee at least a few hours of each day in which students aren't inundated with text messages and notifications from social media apps.

FINDING SOLUTIONS

Over time, more and more teachers, parents, school administrators, researchers, and civic leaders have brought attention to issues such as cell phone use in schools, the right age to get a smartphone, online privacy, and cyberbullying. Some technology companies are stepping up too. In 2018, Apple introduced digital-wellness features that would help users take control of their screen time by setting time limits, monitoring time spent on apps, muting notifications, and more. These tools also give parents more options when it comes to managing their children's devices.

Other companies are taking action as well. Google released digital-wellness tools called Digital Wellbeing for its Android devices. Similar to Apple's features, these tools track phone app usage and allow users to set limits.

According to Maggie Stanphill, user experience director at Digital Wellbeing, "Our devices should help support our intentions throughout the day. Whether it's work, school, or family and friends that we want to focus on, our devices shouldn't get in the way."[2]

In 2019, Instagram released tools intended to help reduce online harassment. Instagram researchers found that teenagers didn't usually block bullies on the platform. This was in part because blocking someone could potentially escalate the situation, as the person being blocked is notified. The other issue is that the victim could not see the bully's posts once the victim blocked the bully. This meant the bully could continue posting harassing content without the victim knowing. The new feature, called Restrict, allows users to restrict comments and messages from cyberbullies. When a bully comments on a person's post, the person must approve the comment before it appears. Messages from the bully go into a separate inbox. Of the new features, Mosseri

"BUT FOR EVERY YOUNG PERSON HUNCHED OVER A SCREEN, THERE ARE OTHERS FOR WHOM SOCIAL MEDIA NO LONGER HOLDS SUCH AN ALLURE. THESE TEENS ARE TURNING THEIR BACKS ON THE TECHNOLOGY—AND THERE ARE MORE OF THEM THAN YOU MIGHT THINK."[3]
—*SIRIN KALE, THE* GUARDIAN, *2018*

QUITTING FACEBOOK

As social media continues to cause stress in their lives, some people are opting out by taking breaks from or permanently deleting social media apps. In 2018, the Pew Research Center conducted a survey of US adults who use Facebook. Approximately 42 percent of respondents said they have taken a break from checking Facebook for at least several weeks, and 26 percent reported having deleted the app from their cell phone. The study also found that younger users, ages 18 to 29, were much more likely to have deleted the app. Only 12 percent of users ages 65 and older had deleted the app, while 44 percent of younger users had made the change.[5] The survey was undertaken following news that a consulting firm had collected data from Facebook users without their knowledge and used it primarily for political advertising. The 2018 scandal sparked debates about privacy, data misuse, and what responsibility Facebook has to protect its users.

said, "[Restrict] gives a target of bullying a bit more power over the experience."[4] In addition to these antibullying features, Instagram has taken further steps to curb harmful posts on the platform, banning content that shows self-harm and limiting posts about diet products and cosmetic surgery.

Some nonprofit organizations offer guidance for using social media and the internet. They help not only parents and teachers but also teens. Common Sense Media does research, reviews apps and other forms of media, offers advice, and advocates for responsible social media use. Its Digital Citizenship Curriculum was one of the first K–12 programs to help students take control of their digital lives. In 2019, the organization released a revamped version of the curriculum that aims to help students as they "navigate a fast-changing digital terrain fraught with hate speech, cyberbullying, fake media and constant digital distraction."[6] It also advocates for laws that support kids' and teens' privacy online.

In 2016, the organization introduced Device-Free Dinner, an initiative aimed at promoting healthier use of personal devices. Michael Robb, the director of research at Common Sense Media,

SIGNS OF STRESS

In 2014, researchers at Tsinghua University in Beijing, China, embarked on a series of experiments to see whether social media sites could detect stress levels based on the content users post. The authors said, "With the popularity of social media, people are used to sharing their daily activities and interacting with friends on social media platforms, making it feasible to leverage online social network data for stress detection."[7] They are working on network models that could automatically detect psychological stress using tweets, texts, images, and other online interactions. By analyzing the user's language, times of day when the user is posting, and other attributes, the model may one day help individuals and mental health agencies detect when a person is feeling stressed or otherwise psychologically unwell.

Initiatives such as Device-Free Dinner encourage people to spend more time with family and less time on screens.

said, "In the digital age, it's easy to let devices occupy more and more of our family time. As more kids and parents bring their devices to the table, we wonder if a prime opportunity to connect with family without distractions is getting lost."[8] Common Sense Media hopes that a device-free mealtime can help people tune back into time with family and friends.

TURNING A NEGATIVE INTO A POSITIVE

Social media doesn't have to waste time, produce stress, or be a negative part of life. In fact, at its best, social media and the digital world can help people feel more connected, supported, and included. Through social media apps, users meet people who will change their lives and join communities that have a positive impact on both individuals and the world. Social media is a place for organizing politically and socially, gathering information, creating, and making voices heard. According to a 2018 survey from the Pew Research Center, about 45 percent of surveyed teens believe social media has neither a positive nor negative impact on people in their age group. Around 31 percent said it has a positive effect, and 24 percent said the overall impact of social media on teens is negative.[9]

"BY RELATIVELY LARGE MARGINS, TEENS INDICATE THAT SOCIAL MEDIA MAKES THEM FEEL INCLUDED RATHER THAN EXCLUDED (71 PERCENT VS. 25 PERCENT), CONFIDENT RATHER THAN INSECURE (69 PERCENT VS. 26 PERCENT), AUTHENTIC RATHER THAN FAKE (64 PERCENT VS. 33 PERCENT), AND OUTGOING RATHER THAN RESERVED (61 PERCENT VS. 34 PERCENT)."[10]

—PEW RESEARCH CENTER, 2018

Though social media has the power to create stress and have a negative impact on users' lives, it also has the power to lift people up and produce positivity. One of the respondents to the 2018 survey, a 15-year-old girl, reflected, "I feel that social media can make people my age feel less lonely or alone. It creates a space where you can interact with people." Another respondent, a 15-year-old boy, said, "It enables people to connect with friends easily and be able to make new friends as well."[11]

While policymakers, tech companies, teachers, and parents have some say in the social media realm, individuals have their own relationships to social media and the digital world and can decide the power they will have in their lives. The more users can utilize media consciously—taking breaks and not engaging in cyberbullying, among other things—the more positive the online experience will be. When the tide turns from endless, zombielike scrolling and trolling online to positive, occasional socializing that is second to experiencing life in person, that's when balance can be found.

A healthy relationship with technology and digital devices is essential to living a happy life.

ESSENTIAL FACTS

FACTS ABOUT SOCIAL MEDIA AND DIGITAL STRESS

- US teens average seven hours and 22 minutes of screen time each day. This does not include time spent using screens at school or for homework.

- Moderate and high amounts of screen time have been linked to anxiety, depression, and emotional instability in teenagers.

- About 3.8 billion people are active social media users. Most of them access social media apps through mobile phones.

IMPACT ON DAILY LIFE

- Social media and digital devices can be both distracting and addictive.

- Screen time and mobile phone use have been linked to sleep problems.

- Signs and symptoms of stress can include stomachaches, headaches, general body aches, feelings of anxiety, panic attacks, anger, and family conflicts, among other things.

- Research shows that too much social media use can negatively affect a person's mental health.

- Fear of missing out (FOMO) can cause users to check their devices and social media feeds on a near-constant basis.

DEALING WITH SOCIAL MEDIA AND DIGITAL STRESS

- Digital-wellness features can help users take control of their screen time.
- Turning off notifications, restricting app usage, and taking breaks are steps that can help reduce social media stress.
- Parents, teachers, counselors, and other trusted adults are important allies when it comes to dealing with social media and digital stress.

QUOTE

"I most definitely see the connection between higher levels of stress and being on your phone for a more than needed amount of time. Scrolling through social media and looking at small square sized snapshots of a person's 'picture perfect life' can really have an effect on both self-esteem and mental health."

—Sadie Dunne for the New York Times, *2020*

GLOSSARY

addiction
A compulsive need for a habit-forming substance, activity, or behavior

auditory cue
A sound signal that a person is meant to hear and interpret.

chronic stress
A constant or nearly constant state of heightened alertness that causes symptoms such as fatigue, headaches, and digestive problems.

cold turkey
Abruptly and completely; most often used with *quit*.

empathy
Being able to understand and share another person's thoughts and feelings.

hack
To secretly get access to the files on a computer or network in order to get information or cause damage.

HTML

Hypertext Markup Language, a basic computer language that allows users to build and structure web pages.

notification

An icon, sound, message, or similar alert sent by a mobile device app.

post-traumatic stress

A mental and physical state brought on by a traumatic event and usually characterized by irritability, anxiety, depression, and insomnia.

psychopathology

Psychological and behavioral dysfunction related to mental disorders.

wearable

A smart electronic device, such as a watch, bracelet, or step tracker, that can be worn.

ADDITIONAL RESOURCES

SELECTED BIBLIOGRAPHY

Anderson, Monica, and Jingjing Jiang. "Teens' Social Media Habits and Experiences." *Pew Research Center*, 28 Nov. 2018, pewresearch.org. Accessed 21 May 2020.

Rideout, Victoria, and Michael B. Robb. *The Common Sense Census.* Common Sense Media, 2019.

Twenge, Jean M. "Have Smartphones Destroyed a Generation?" *Atlantic*, Sept. 2017, theatlantic.com. Accessed 21 May 2020.

FURTHER READINGS

Huddleston, Emma. *Using Social Media Responsibly.* Abdo, 2021.

Marciniak, Kristin. *Twitter.* Abdo, 2019.

Mooney, Carla. *Addicted to Social Media.* ReferencePoint, 2019.

ONLINE RESOURCES

Booklinks
NONFICTION NETWORK
FREE! ONLINE NONFICTION RESOURCES

To learn more about social media and digital stress, please visit **abdobooklinks.com** or scan this QR code. These links are routinely monitored and updated to provide the most current information available.

MORE INFORMATION

For more information on this subject, contact or visit the following organizations:

Common Sense Media

699 Eighth St., Ste. C150
San Francisco, CA 94103
415-863-0600
commonsensemedia.org

Common Sense Media provides research-backed information and education for the digital world. Its website offers reviews of movies, books, apps, and games.

StopBullying.gov

US Department of Health and Human Services
200 Independence Ave. SW
Washington, DC 20201
877-696-6775
stopbullying.gov

This federal government resource offers advice for those who are being bullied or cyberbullied.

SOURCE NOTES

CHAPTER 1. TECHNOLOGY OVERLOAD

1. Jean M. Twenge. "Have Smartphones Destroyed a Generation?" *Atlantic*, Sept. 2017, theatlantic.com. Accessed 13 Aug. 2020.
2. "The Common Sense Census: Media Use by Tweens and Teens, 2019." *Common Sense Media*, n.d., commonsensemedia.org. Accessed 13 Aug. 2020.
3. "The Common Sense Census: Media Use by Tweens and Teens, 2019."
4. Jean M. Twenge and W. Keith Campbell. "Associations Between Screen Time and Lower Psychological Well-Being among Children and Adolescents." *Preventive Medicine Reports*, Dec. 2018, sciencedirect.com. Accessed 13 Aug. 2020.
5. "The Common Sense Census: Media Use by Tweens and Teens, 2019."
6. "New Study: Reduced Screen Time for Young Highly Recommended For Wellbeing." *EurekAlert*, 29 Oct. 2018, eurekalert.com. Accessed 13 Aug. 2020.
7. Carrie James et al. "Teaching Digital Citizens in Today's World: Research and Insights behind the Common Sense K–12 Digital Citizenship Curriculum." *Common Sense Media*, 2019, commonsense.org. Accessed 13 Aug. 2020.

CHAPTER 2. WHAT IS DIGITAL STRESS?

1. Monica Anderson and Jingjing Jiang. "Teens, Social Media & Technology 2018." *Pew Research Center*, 31 May 2018, pewresearch.org. Accessed 13 Aug. 2020.
2. "Mobile Fact Sheet." *Pew Research Center*, 12 June 2019, pewresearch.org. Accessed 13 Aug. 2020.
3. Goali Saedi Bocci. *The Social Media Workbook for Teens: Skills to Help You Balance Screen Time, Manage Stress, and Take Charge of Your Life*. New Harbinger, 2019. viii.
4. Markham Heid. "Experts Say 'How Much' Is the Wrong Way to Assess Screen Time." *Time*, 29 May 2019, time.com. Accessed 13 Aug. 2020.
5. Markham Heid. "You Asked: Is Social Media Making Me Miserable?" *Time*, 2 Aug. 2017, time.com. Accessed 13 Aug. 2020.
6. Antonio-Manuel Rodríguez-García et al. "Nomophobia: An Individual's Growing Fear of Being without a Smartphone." *International Journal of Environmental Research and Public Health*, 16 Jan. 2020, mdpi.com. Accessed 13 Aug. 2020.
7. Seunghee Han, Ki Joon Kim, and Jang Hyun Kim. "Understanding Nomophobia." *Cyberpsychology, Behavior and Social Networking*, 1 July 2017, liebertpub.com. Accessed 13 Aug. 2020.
8. "Anxiety." *APA*, 2020, apa.org. Accessed 5 Apr. 2020.
9. Milena Foerster et al. "Impact of Adolescents' Screen Time and Nocturnal Mobile Phone–Related Awakenings on Sleep and General Health Symptoms." *International Journal of Environmental Research and Public Health*, 12 Feb. 2019, mdpi.com. Accessed 13 Aug. 2020.

CHAPTER 3. SOCIAL MEDIA HISTORY

1. "25 Years Since the World's First Text Message." *Vodafone*, 4 Dec. 2017, vodafone.com. Accessed 13 Aug. 2020.
2. "Social Media Fact Sheet." *Pew Research Center*, 12 June 2019, pewresearch.org. Accessed 13 Aug. 2020.
3. "Timeline of Computer History." *Computer History Museum*, 2020, computerhistory.org. Accessed 22 June 2020.

4. J. Clement. "Global Digital Population as of July 2020." *Statista*, 24 July 2020, statista.com. Accessed 13 Aug. 2020.
5. "30 Years On, What's Next #ForTheWeb?" *World Wide Web Foundation*, 12 Mar. 2019, webfoundation.org. Accessed 13 Aug. 2020.
6. Dave Chaffey. "Global Social Media Research Summary July 2020." *Smart Insights*, 3 Aug. 2020, smartinsights.com. Accessed 13 Aug. 2020.
7. The Learning Network. "What Students Are Saying about How Much They Use Their Phones, and Whether We Should Be Worried." *New York Times*, 6 Feb. 2020, nytimes.com. Accessed 13 Aug. 2020.
8. "7 Social Media Sites that Failed to Become 'Facebook.'" *Economic Times*, 28 May 2017, economictimes.indiatimes.com. Accessed 13 Aug. 2020.
9. Lori Kozlowski. "New Life: How MySpace Spawned a Start-Up Ecosystem." *Forbes*, 15 May 2012, forbes.com. Accessed 13 Aug. 2020.
10. David Pierce. "Even Steve Jobs Didn't Predict the iPhone Decade." *Wired*, 9 Jan. 2017, wired.com. Accessed 13 Aug. 2020.
11. Anthony Wing Kosner. "Tim Cook Again Expresses Intense Interest in TV Market, but Mutes the Real Issues." *Forbes*, 7 Dec. 2012, forbes.com. Accessed 13 Aug. 2020.

CHAPTER 4. YOUTH, YOUNG ADULTS, AND DIGITAL STRESS

1. Michael Lynch. "Leave My iPhone Alone: Why Our Smartphones Are Extensions of Ourselves." *Guardian*, 19 Feb. 2016, theguardian.com. Accessed 13 Aug. 2020.
2. Jean M. Twenge. "Have Smartphones Destroyed a Generation?" *Atlantic*, Sept. 2017, theatlantic.com. Accessed 13 Aug. 2020.
3. "Protect Your Brain from Stress." *Harvard Health Publishing*, Aug. 2018, health.harvard.edu. Accessed 13 Aug. 2020.
4. Melina R. Uncapher et al. "Media Multitasking and Cognitive, Psychological, Neural, and Learning Differences." *Pediatrics*, Nov. 2017, pediatrics.aappublications.org. Accessed 13 Aug. 2020.
5. Melina R. Uncapher and Anthony D. Wagner. "Minds and Brains of Media Multitaskers: Current Findings and Future Directions." *PNAS*, 2 Oct. 2018, pnas.org. Accessed 13 Aug. 2020.
6. Chandni Sheth et al. "Chronic Stress in Adolescents and Its Neurobiological and Psychopathological Consequences." *Chronic Stress*, 18 June 2017, pubmed.ncbi.nlm.nih.gov. Accessed 13 Aug. 2020.
7. The Learning Network. "What Students Are Saying about How Much They Use Their Phones, and Whether We Should Be Worried." *New York Times*, 6 Feb. 2020, nytimes.com. Accessed 13 Aug. 2020.
8. Eveline A. Crone and Elly A. Konijn. "Media Use and Brain Development during Adolescence." *Nature Communications*, 21 Feb. 2018, nature.com. Accessed 13 Aug. 2020.
9. "The Common Sense Census: Media Use by Tweens and Teens, 2019." *Common Sense Media*, n.d., commonsensemedia.org. Accessed 13 Aug. 2020.

CHAPTER 5. SOCIAL MEDIA STRESS

1. Alexandra Samuel. "With Social Media, Everyone's a Celebrity." *JSTOR Daily*, 16 July 2019, daily.jstor.org. Accessed 13 Aug. 2020.
2. "Body Dysmorphic Disorder." *Mayo Clinic*, 29 Oct. 2019, mayoclinic.org. Accessed 13 Aug. 2020.

3. "Do Tweens and Teens Believe 'Fake News'?" *Common Sense Media*, n.d., commonsensemedia.org. Accessed 10 Apr. 2020.

4. Emily Stewart. "People over 65 Are the Most Likely to Share Fake News on Facebook, Study Finds." *Vox*, 10 Jan. 2019, vox.com. Accessed 13 Aug. 2020.

5. Emily Shugerman. "Logan Paul Apology: Read It in Full." *Independent*, 3 Jan. 2018, independent.co.uk. Accessed 13 Aug. 2020.

6. Paige Cooper. "Want to Buy Instagram Followers? Here's What Happens When You Do." *Hootsuite*, 15 Oct. 2019, blog.hootsuite.com. Accessed 13 Aug. 2020.

7. The Learning Network. "What Students Are Saying about How Much They Use Their Phones, and Whether We Should Be Worried." *New York Times*, 6 Feb. 2020, nytimes.com. Accessed 13 Aug. 2020.

8. John Herrman. "How Tiny Red Dots Took Over Your Life." *New York Times Magazine*, 27 Feb. 2018, nytimes.com. Accessed 13 Aug. 2020.

9. Amanda Lenhart. "Teens, Technology, and Friendships." *Pew Research Center*, 6 Aug. 2015, pewresearch.org. Accessed 13 Aug. 2020.

CHAPTER 6. NEGATIVITY ONLINE

1. Ainoa Mateu et al. "Cyberbullying and Post-Traumatic Stress Symptoms in UK Adolescents." *Archives of Disease in Childhood*, 23 June 2020, adc.bmj.com. Accessed 13 Aug. 2020.

2. Justin W. Patchin. "2019 Cyberbullying Data." *Cyberbullying Research Center*, 9 July 2019, cyberbullying.org. Accessed 13 Apr. 2020.

3. Monica Anderson. "A Majority of Teens Have Experienced Some Form of Cyberbullying." *Pew Research Center*, 27 Sept. 2018, pewresearch.org. Accessed 13 Aug. 2020.

4. Emma Grey Ellis. "Swatting Is a Deadly Problem—Here's the Solution." *Wired*, 22 Aug. 2019, wired.com. Accessed 21 Sept. 2020.

5. Taylor Lorenz. "Teens Are Being Bullied 'Constantly' on Instagram." *Atlantic*, 10 Oct. 2018, theatlantic.com. Accessed 13 Aug. 2020.

6. Anderson, "A Majority of Teens Have Experienced Some Form of Cyberbullying."

7. USC School of Social Work staff. "Stalking in the Age of Social Media." *USC News*, 19 Feb. 2018, news.usc.edu. Accessed 13 Aug. 2020.

8. Juli Fraga. "When Teens Cyberbully Themselves." *NPR*, 21 Apr. 2018, npr.org. Accessed 13 Aug. 2020.

9. USC School of Social Work staff, "Stalking in the Age of Social Media."

10. "11 Facts about Cyberbullying." *DoSomething.org*, n.d., dosomething.org. Accessed 5 Apr. 2020.

CHAPTER 7. DISTRACTION, ADDICTION, AND EMOTIONAL CONSEQUENCES

1. "New Study Shows Wearable Technology Also Contributes to Distracted Driving." *ScienceDaily*, 23 Apr. 2018, sciencedaily.com. Accessed 25 June 2020.

2. Jingjing Jiang. "How Teens and Parents Navigate Screen Time and Device Distractions." *Pew Research Center*, 22 Aug. 2018, pewresearch.org. Accessed 13 Aug. 2020.

3. Hilarie Cash. "Why Is It So Hard to Believe in a Behavioral Addiction?" *Psychology Today*, 20 Nov. 2011, psychologytoday.com. Accessed 13 Aug. 2020.

4. Mark Griffiths and Daria Kuss. "6 Questions Help Reveal If You're Addicted to Social Media." *Washington Post*, 25 Apr. 2018, washingtonpost.com. Accessed 13 Aug. 2020.

5. "Technology Addiction: Concern, Controversy, and Finding Balance." *Common Sense Media*, n.d., commonsensemedia.org. Accessed 13 Aug. 2020.
6. "Dealing with Digital Distraction." *APA*, 10 Aug. 2018, apa.org. Accessed 13 Aug. 2020.
7. Jaime E. Sidani et al. "The Association between Social Media Use and Eating Concerns among US Young Adults." *Journal of the Academy of Nutrition and Dietetics*, 5 May 2016, ncbi.nlm.nih.gov. Accessed 13 Aug. 2020.

CHAPTER 8. OVERCOMING DIGITAL AND SOCIAL MEDIA STRESS

1. "Taking a Technology Break Can Help Your Health." *UW Health*, 26 Apr. 2019, uwhealth.org. Accessed 13 Aug. 2020.
2. Colleen Leahy. "Expert: Moderation Is Key with Social Media and Here Is How To Do That." *Wisconsin Public Radio*, 11 Aug. 2017, wpr.org. Accessed 13 Aug. 2020.
3. Katherine Schaeffer. "Most U.S. Teens Who Use Cell Phones Do It to Pass Time, Connect with Others, Learn New Things." *Pew Research Center*, 23 Aug. 2019, pewresearch-org-prepod.go-vip.co. Accessed 13 Aug. 2020.
4. Airen Petalbert. "How to Take a Social Media Detox without Deleting Your Accounts." *Tech Times*, 23 Dec. 2019, techtimes.com. Accessed 13 Aug. 2020.
5. Carolyn Thompson. "Schools Reckon with Social Stress: 'I'm on My Phone So Much.'" *NBC Washington*, 7 June 2019, nbcwashington.com. Accessed 13 Aug. 2020.
6. Jennifer Guttman. "6 Ways to Detox and Cleanse Your Social Media Usage." *Psychology Today*, 3 Jan. 2020, psychologytoday.com. Accessed 13 Aug. 2020.
7. Jason Zook. "What I Learned from a 30-Day Social Media Detox." *Wandering Aimfully*, n.d., wanderingaimfully.com. Accessed 24 June 2020.

CHAPTER 9. FINDING A BALANCE

1. Aubri Juhasz. "Instagram Now Lets You Control Your Bully's Comments." *NPR*, 3 Oct. 2019, npr.org. Accessed 13 Aug. 2020.
2. Maggie Stanphill. "Find Your Balance with New Digital Wellbeing Tools." *Google*, 14 May 2019, blog.google. Accessed 13 Aug. 2020.
3. Sirin Kale. "Logged Off: Meet the Teens Who Refuse to Use Social Media." *Guardian*, 29 Aug. 2018, theguardian.com. Accessed 13 Aug. 2020.
4. Juhasz, "Instagram Now Lets You Control Your Bully's Comments."
5. Andrew Perrin. "Americans Are Changing Their Relationships with Facebook." *Pew Research Center*, 5 Sept. 2018, pewresearch.org. Accessed 13 Aug. 2020.
6. "Revamped Common Sense Digital Citizenship Curriculum Now Complete and Addresses Urgent Emerging Needs." *Common Sense Media*, 12 Aug. 2019, commonsensemedia.org. Accessed 13 Aug. 2020.
7. Huijie Lin et al. "Detecting Stress Based on Social Interactions in Social Networks." *IEEE*, 1 Sept. 2017, ieeexplore.ieee.org. Accessed 13 Aug. 2020.
8. Michael Robb. "Why Device-Free Dinners Are a Healthy Choice." *Common Sense Media*, 4 Aug. 2016, commonsensemedia.org. Accessed 13 Aug. 2020.
9. Monica Anderson and Jingjing Jiang. "Teens, Social Media & Technology 2018." *Pew Research Center*, 31 May 2018, pewresearch.org. Accessed 13 Aug. 2020.
10. Monica Anderson and Jingjing Jiang. "Teens' Social Media Habits and Experiences." *Pew Research Center*, 28 Nov. 2018, pewresearch.org. Accessed 13 Aug. 2020.
11. Anderson and Jiang, "Teens, Social Media & Technology 2018."

INDEX

ABOUT THE AUTHOR

KAITLYN DULING

Kaitlyn Duling believes in the power of words to change hearts, minds, and actions. An avid reader and writer who grew up in Illinois, she now resides in Washington, DC. She knows that knowledge of the past is the key to our future and wants to ensure that all children and families have access to high-quality information. Duling has written over one hundred books for children and teens.

ABOUT THE CONSULTANT

DR. MARGUERITE OHRTMAN

Dr. Marguerite Ohrtman is an assistant professor, director of school counseling, and director of clinical training at the University of Minnesota's Counselor Education program. She received her doctoral and master's degrees in counselor education and supervision from Minnesota State University, Mankato. She is a former classroom teacher and a licensed school counselor and professional clinical counselor in Minnesota. In addition, Ohrtman supervises counselors, counsels clients in private practice, and serves as a consultant to school districts. Ohrtman is the past president of the Minnesota State Counselor Association and has published and presented on various school counseling topics.